COMPULSORY

This Land ... This Terror

Script/Inks: Comrade Barr
Pencils: Domski Regan
Lettering: Pioter Rorkov

Ghost Ship of the Reich

Script: Comrade Barr
Pencils/Inks/Lettering: Zielkov Kirbloski

This State Divided

Script: Comrade Barr
Pencils/Lettering: Domski Regan
Pencils Lackey: Kurt Siblomov
Inks: Alexander Davidovich

Battling Barbarians From Beyond

Script: Comrade Barr
Pencils/Inks/Lettering:Domski Regan

Poster Art by Comrade Barr and Zielkov Kirbloski
Hand of Lenin Proofing by Pioter Rorkov
Edited and co-created by Igor Sloano and Comrade Barr

REPRINT CREDITS:

PUBLISHER: Ed Murphy
BOOK DESIGN: Jim Cunningham
EDITORIAL ASSISTANT: Jane McLelland

EDITOR: Tom Campbell
COVER DESIGN: Derek Dow

REPRINT ARTISTS: Dave Alexander, Colin Barr, De
Dominic Regan and Curt Sibling. Special tha

THE FREEDOM COLLECTIVE is published by **KREMLIN COMICS, OFFICE OF PUBLICATION, THE KREMLIN, MOSCOW.** Published by The State for the benefit and education of its readers. All rights reserved. No similarity between any of the names, characters, persons - either living, dead or in exile within far-flung regions - and institutions is intended and any such similiarities which may exist is purely coincidental. Although it may be said to symbolise the glorious struggles of the workers and the State against the corrupt capitalist democracies who threaten to overwhelm and enslave us all. Why are you reading this text this small? Are you some kind of subversive who pries into matters that are not their business? Perhaps you think to question the will of The State? If so, report yourself immediately and remember that The State is ALWAYS beyond question. Reprinted in the corrupt democracies by **ROUGH CUT COMICS.**BAH!

OUR STORY STARTS AS ALWAYS IN THAT CITADEL OF LIBERTY *THE KREMLIN!* WHERE OUR MOST HONOURED LEADER ADDRESSES OUR HEROES, THE *KRIMSON KOMMISSAR, AJYS, HOMELAND, MIKHAIL MOLOTOV (MIG-4)* AND *VLADIMIR VERASHAKIN (MASTODON)*.

GREETINGS ESTEEMED COMRADES, I HAVE CALLED YOU HERE ON A MATTER OF *UTMOST URGENCY!*

THIS IS *BORIS STAVROGIN,* ONE OF OUR RESEARCH SCIENTISTS. HE VANISHED WITH HIS FAMILY TWO DAYS AGO!

HIS COLLEAGUES REPORTED A GROWING FASCINATION WITH AMERICAN *DECADENCE* AND *LIES* AND WE NOW BELIEVE THAT HE HAS *DEFECTED* TO THE WEST! CONCERNED FOR HIS WELFARE, THE KGB ARRANGED TO *INTERVIEW* HIM, BUT HE NEVER KEPT THE *APPOINTMENT!*

EVIDENCE SUGGESTS THAT HE AND HIS FAMILY WERE PICKED UP BY A SUBMARINE AT THE COAST AND ARE NOW IN THE HANDS OF ...*THE CHIEF!!*

THE CHIEF! HOW THAT NAME SENDS A SHUDDER DOWN EVEN MY ICY SPINE!

I CANNOT STRESS HOW IMPORTANT IT IS TO RESCUE THESE PEOPLE! STAVROGIN IS A MINOR SCIENTIST. HE CAN CONTRIBUTE LITTLE TO THE WEST'S ARSENAL OF *STOLEN* SECRETS! BUT IT IS HIS *FAMILY...*

...THOSE POOR PEOPLE DO NOT DESERVE TO *SUFFER* FOR STAVROGIN'S SELFISH STUPIDITY! THE THOUGHT OF THEM IN THE HANDS OF THAT *BEAST!* I...I HOLD MYSELF PERSONALLY RESPONSIBLE FOR THEM!

DO NOT BLAME YOURSELF COMRADE, THERE WAS NO WAY YOU COULD HAVE FORESEEN THIS BETRAYAL!

PERHAPS SO, BUT THIS IS NO TIME FOR *SLACKING,* YOUR MISSION IS TO RESCUE STAVROGIN AND HIS FAMILY! EVEN IF YOU MUST BRAVE THE VERY DEPTHS OF THAT CAPITALIST *DUNGEON* TO DO SO!!

2

BUT NOW LET US JOURNEY ACROSS THE GLOBE TO THAT PARTICULAR CAPITALIST *DUNGEON*, WHERE A MENACING FIGURE IS DISHING OUT HIS *USUAL* ROUND OF THREATS...

YOU HEARD *FUZZFACE*!! GIT *DEM* MISSILES OFF A DAT ISLAND OR YOU *WON'T* KNOW WHAT HIT YA!!

WHO CARES IF IT *AIN'T* AMERICAN SOIL, I'M *DA CHIEF* AN' WHAT I SEZ GOES!!

HAW! THAT'LL TEACH THEM COMMIES TO TRY AN' *PROTECT* THEMSELVES, AIN'T NOBODY PACKS *MORE* MISSILES THAN *DA CHIEF!*.. AIN'T THAT *RIGHT*, VON BRAUN?

HEH! HEH! HOW COULD YOU BE *WRONG* MEIN CHIEF?

YOU BETTER BELIEVE IT BUB! REMEMBER YA *OWE* ME FOR GETTIN' YOUR BUDDIES OUTTA THAT BUNKER!

WHICH IS WHY THEY HAFF SENT ME TO WORK WITH YOU! AFTER ALL WE SHARE THE *SAME* GOALS!

IZZAT SO? WELL MEBBE YOU BETTER PUT YOUR MONEY WHERE YOUR MOUTH IS! I WANT RESULTS ON PROJECT *DEAD RED!* AN' I WANT 'EM AS IN YESTERDAY!

UND YOU SHALL *HAFF* THEM! EVERYTHING IS *ALMOST* READY!

ALMOST AIN'T *GOOD* ENUFF!! WORD IS THE FREEDOM COLLECTIVE'S ON THEIR WAY TA' RESCUE THAT SCIENTIST WE *CONNED!*..ER *PERSUADED* INTA' JOININ' US!

THEN THEY RUSH INTO THE JAWS OF A *TRAP*, COME! A TOAST, CHIEF, TO OUR JOINT EFFORTS!

YEAH! HERE'S TA *TEAMWORK* OL' BUD!

CREEP'S GETTIN' TOO BIG FOR HIS BOOTS! GONNA' HAVE TA' STRING HIM ALONG FOR A WHILE, THEN RUB 'IM OUT WHILE HIS BACK'S TURNED!

TO *TEAMWORK!* UND CRUSHING THOSE IDEALISTIC FOOLS!

ENJOY IT WHILE YOU CAN, AMERICAN PIG! SOON YOUR WHITE HOUSE WILL *BOW* TO A *NEW* REICH!

3

HAH! LOOKS LIKE THE BOYS HERE ARE GONNA HAVE A LITTLE *SURPRISE* FOR THEM BOZO'S WHEN THEY SHOW THEIR FACES!!

'CEPT FOR THE KOMMISSAR... HE'S *MINE* I GOT ME EVERYTHING I *NEED* TA DEAL WITH THAT PANTYWAIST *HERE!*...

...AN *HERE!!*

THOOM!

LATER THAT DAY, A SUBMARINE DOCKS AT A PORT IN THE HAVEN OF *CUBA* AND OUR HEROES DISEMBARK!

WELCOME TO OUR SHORES, ALL OF YOU!

"AHHH!!...IT IS GOOD...TO TOUCH ...COMMUNIST SOIL...AGAIN!"

HOMELAND SPEAKS FOR US *ALL* OUR LEADER SENDS HIS REGARDS, COMRADE *CASTRO!*

...OUR INTELLIGENCE CONFIRMS THAT STAVROGIN IS IMPRISONED DEEP WITHIN THE WHITE HOUSE ITSELF. RESCUING HIM SHOULD PROVE NO MEAN FEAT, *EVEN* FOR YOU FIVE!

HUH! WE'RE *NOT* AFRAID OF THAT YANKEE GORILLA OR HIS LACKEYS...

"ONCE I *FIRE UP,* I'LL FLY *RINGS* AROUND THEM SO FAST THAT THEY'LL BLACKOUT FROM DIZZINESS!"

"SO WHAT? WHEN I CHANGE INTO *MASTODON* I'LL *UPROOT* THAT CORRUPT WHITE HOUSE FROM IT'S VERY FOUNDATIONS! SEE WHAT THE CHIEF *THINKS* OF THAT!"

YOUR INTENTIONS ARE LAUDABLE, COMRADES! BUT NEVER FORGET THAT THE AMERICANS ARE A *CUNNING* AND *DANGEROUS* FOE!

HE'S *RIGHT,* COMRADES...

4

"REMEMBER THE DASTARDLY *U2* SPYPLANE AFFAIR! WHEN THE AMERICANS SECRETLY *SPIED* ON US FROM THE VERY EDGES OF *SPACE* ONLY TO BE UNDONE BY *MASTODON'S* ABILITY TO TAKE GARGANTUAN LEAPS!"

HAW! WAIT TILL THE GUYS GET A LOAD OF *THESE* PICS, HEY WUZZAT?...NO! NO!!!

"...AND BEFORE THAT, WHEN OUR LEADER HIMSELF JOURNEYED TO AMERICA FOR A *"PEACEFUL VISIT"* AT THE INVITATION OF THE CHIEF'S BRUTAL PREDECESSOR..."

YA *FELL* FOR IT! BOYS *GRAB* HIM!

YOU TAKE US FOR FOOLS? WE WERE *WISE* TO THIS TRAP!

WHAT DO YOU MEAN BY-- AWWW NO! HE'S JUST A *CRUMMY ROBOT!!*

YOU WILL *NEVER* CRUSH FREEDOM SO LONG AS ONE COMMUNIST DRAWS BREATH! FAREWELL COMRADE!

AFTER REFRESHING THEMSELVES, THE COLLECTIVE DON CIVILIAN DISGUISES AND EMBARK ON THE LAST LEG OF THEIR *PERILOUS* JOURNEY!

THESE RAGS SHOULD ALLOW YOU TO BLEND IN WITH THE REST OF THE SO-CALLED REFUGEES!

I...I DON'T UNDERSTAND, *WHY* ARE THEY LEAVING YOUR COUNTRY FOR AMERICA?

THE POOR FOOLS ACTUALLY *BELIEVE* THE CHIEF'S LIES ABOUT THE LAND OF MILK AND HONEY! ...PERHAPS IT IS BETTER THIS WAY, FOR ONLY THE *WEAK* AND THE *TREACHEROUS* CRAVE SUCH DECADENCE!

YEAH! LIKE THAT *RAT* STAVROGIN, WHEN I GET MY ...

NO, MIG-4!

COMRADE STAVROGIN IS A *CITIZEN* OF OUR COUNTRY AND AS SUCH IS ENTITLED TO *FAIR* TREATMENT!

BESIDES, I SUSPECT THAT THE CHIEF'S *HOSPITALITY* HAS BEEN PUNISHMENT ENOUGH!

GOOD POINT, KOMMISSAR!

WHICH IS WHY I WILL *NEVER* ALLOW SUCH TYRANNY TO BLACKEN OUR SHORES!

5

AND THEY ARE IN *GOOD* HANDS, FAREWELL!

IT HAS BEEN AN HONOUR...

NO COMRADE. THE *HONOUR* IS OURS!

A LONE MAN STANDING BETWEEN HIS PEOPLE AND A NATION OF UTTER TYRANNY! SOMETIMES, COMRADE, I AM REMINDED WHO THE *REAL* HEROES ARE!

BUT THERE ARE THOSE WHOSE THOUGHTS THOUGH NOBLE, ARE ALSO *WEAKENED* BY SENTIMENTALITY...

AJYS I SENSE ...YOUR *PAIN!* WHY DO YOU ... NOT TELL THE KOMMISSAR...YOUR FEELINGS FOR HIM?

NO...HOMELAND! IT WOULD BE SELFISH! I WOULD BE PLACING MYSELF *ABOVE* OTHERS!

BY THE ETERNAL GLACIERS, HOW COULD I HAVE FORESEEN THAT ONE DAY MY HEART WOULD BELONG TO A MORTAL SWORN TO AN IDEAL...NO, A *TRUTH!!* GREATER THAN EVEN THE *LOVE* OF A GODDESS!

...WHILE THERE ARE STILL OTHERS WHOSE THOUGHTS ARE *NEITHER* SENTIMENTAL OR NOBLE...

HOLY!.. IT'S *THEM!* I'D BETTER WARN THE CHIEF!!

IN THE WHITE HOUSE...

MUNCH! SLOBBER!!... WELL STICK TO'EM, IF YA KNOW WHAT'S *GOOD* FOR YA!

HA! EXCELLENT, I'LL ORDER AN *AIRSTRIKE,* IMMEDIATELY!

WELL *BLOW* THAT BOAT OUTTA —

IDJIT! I TOLD YA, AINT *NOBODY* TOUCHES DEM REDS TILL I SEZ SO!!

THONK!

S'MATTER DUM-DUM, DON'T YA *LIKE* TAKIN ORDERS, MEBBE THINKIN OF MAKING SOME MOVES *BEHIND* MY BACK?

ULP...N..NO WAY, CHIEF!

GLAD TA HEAR IT! NOW PICK UP YOUR BUDDY AN *BEAT* IT!!

6

NIGHTMARE OR NOT, WE HAVE TO FIND SOMEWHERE TO *EAT*.. THAT CAFE LOOKS AS GOOD A PLACE AS ANY!

YES, WE CAN USE THE AMERICAN *MONEY* GIVEN TO US BY COMRADE CASTRO!

*B*UT INSIDE...

WHAT'S THE *PROBLEM*, BOYS?

THIS WISEGUY *AIN'T* SELLIN THE CHIEF'S BOOZE NO MORE. HE SEZ HIS CUSTOMERS *DON'T* LIKE IT!

IT..IT'S *TRUE* IT HAS MADE THEM SICK!

OH, A *TROUBLEMAKER*, EH? LET'S SHOW HIM HOW WE HANDLE HIS KIND HERE!!

THEY'LL *KILL* THAT MAN IF WE DON'T STOP THEM! MIG-4'S RIGHT, WE CAN'T *JUST* STAND BY!

AWRIGHT, BEAT IT YA BUMS! REMEMBER-- YA DIDN'T SEE *NOTHIN*!

THAT GOES FOR YOU *TOO* BUDDY..

...ULP!!

I..AM NOT...YOUR ..*BUDDY*..LITTLE...MAN!

SSKKRAASSHHH!!

...FAR.. FROM...IT!

8

GLANCING INTO THE STREET, *VERASHAKIN* FREEZES AT THE SIGHT OF AN APPROACHING JUGGERNAUT BEING STEERED ON A PATH OF *DESTRUCTION!*

THOSE CREEPS ARE TOO *TOUGH* TA TACKLE BUT THIS OUGHTTA *KNOCK* THE WIND OUTTA THEIR SAILS!!

THEY'RE GOING TO *RAM* THE CAFE ALL THOSE INNOCENT PEOPLE AND THERE'S NO WAY *VLADIMIR VERASHAKIN* CAN STOP THEM!

...BUT MASTODON CAN!!

KA-THOOM!

WHAT WORDS CAN DESCRIBE THE UNUTTERABLE AEONS OLD *FURY* OF MASTODON *UNLEASHED!* THE VERY AIR SHAKES TO HIS *TERRIFYING* ROAR!!!

RRRAAAWW!!

FLEE PUNY MEN MASTODON WILL CHARGE!!!

MEANWHILE *AJYS* AND *HOMELAND* DEAL WITH THEIR ENEMIES AS ONLY THEY CAN...

I...I DON'T BELIEVE IT, IT'S A BLAMED *GLACIER!*

AYE! AND BE THANKFUL WE WILL ONLY USE OUR POWERS TO *IMPRISON* YOU MORTALS!

MASTODON, HEAD FOR THAT ALLEYWAY! THAT'S AN *ORDER!!*

MASTODON'S RAGE *TERRIFIES* ME! WHAT IF HE SHOULD TURN *AGAINST* US ONE DAY... AGAINST THE STATE?

NO!! MASTODON NOT RUN!! MASTODON SMASH!!!

10

THE COLLECTIVE REGROUP AND *MASTODON* UNDERGOES HIS AMAZING TRANSFORMATION BACK INTO *VLADIMIR VERASHAKIN!*

FORGIVE ME *KOMMISSAR,* I...I DID NOT MEAN TO DISOBEY YOUR ORDER! IT'S JUST THAT *MASTODON'S* RAGE SOMETIMES *OVERWHELMS* ME!

WE'LL OVERLOOK IT *THIS* TIME, COMRADE, YOU FOUGHT WELL IN THE FIELD!

I...I OWE YOU MY *LIFE!*

YOU SHOULD NOT BE HERE, COMRADE, IT WOULD BE *DANGEROUS* WERE YOU SEEN WITH US!

WHAT DOES ONE MORE *THREAT* MEAN IN THIS LAND OF *TERROR* AND *BETRAYAL!* I AM INDEBTED TO YOUR COURAGE, MY FRIEND!

HMMM, THEN PERHAPS YOU CAN HELP! IT WILL BE *HARDER* FOR US TO REACH WASHINGTON NOW THAT THEY *KNOW* WE ARE HERE!

THEN FATE HAS SMILED UPON YOU THIS DAY! FOR I HAVE CONTACTS WITH THE *RESISTANCE!* THEY CAN GET YOU THERE!

WITHIN A SHORT TIME OUR HEROES ARE LED THRU A MAZE OF TUNNELS TO A *SECRET* MEETING PLACE!

FRANK! WE THOUGHT THE CHIEFS THUGS *FINISHED* YOU OFF... WAIT! WHO'S THIS...IT...*CAN'T* BE!

BUT IT *IS!* IT'S THE *FREEDOM COLLECTIVE!*

AT EASE, WE COME AS *FRIENDS!*

AFTER INTRODUCTIONS ARE MADE, THE *KOMMISSAR* OUTLINES THE GROUPS SITUATION TO THE RESISTANCE LEADER...

OF COURSE, WE *WILL* HELP YOU! *THE CHIEF* MAY HAVE FORCED FREE MEN TO LIVE DOWN HERE LIKE THIS, BUT HE WILL *NEVER* BREAK OUR SPIRIT!!

MANY THANKS, COMRADE!

AND SO SCANT DAYS LATER, SIX FIGURES *HASTILY* DISEMBARK FROM A TRUCK UNDER THE COVER OF *DARKNESS!*

HERE WE ARE IN *WASHINGTON,* MY FRIENDS, GOOD LUCK!

SO, *THAT'S* IT...

I...SENSE A...GREAT *DARKNESS* ...ABOUT *THAT* PLACE!!...

DARKNESS OR NO DARKNESS, THAT IS *OUR DESTINATION!!*

11

PART 2 — "THE POWER OF THE CHIEF!"

THE WHITE HOUSE! TAKE A GOOD LOOK COMRADES, FEW FREE MEN HAVE EVER SEEN THIS SIGHT WITH THEIR OWN EYES!

BRRR! WHAT A SINISTER PLACE! IT FILLS ME WITH CHILLS!

I'VE HEARD THAT MANY WHO ENTER NEVER RETURN...

WELL I'M NOT GOING TO STAND HERE STARING ALL NIGHT!

LET'S HAVE A CLOSER LOOK... FIRE UP!

WAIT! YOUNG ONE! I THINK THIS FORTRESS MIGHT BEST BE APPROACHED FROM THE OPPOSITE DIRECTION... MASTODON? HOMELAND?

GOOD IDEA KOMMISSAR! MASTODON CAN DIG THROUGH ANYTHING!

AND SO OUR HEROES SET OUT TOWARDS THE MENACING STRUCTURE, THEIR MOVEMENTS HIDDEN BY TONS OF EARTH ABOVE THEM!

WHILE I CAN... COMMAND THE SOIL... TO HARDEN ...AND FORM WALLS... AROUND US!..

12

CAN'T BE MUCH *LONGER* NOW! HOW ARE YOU TWO FARING?

IT IS GETTING *HARDER...* TO MAINTAIN CONTROL. THE SOIL IS...AT IT'S MOST *POISONED*...HERE!

HRRRGH! MASTODON NEVER TIRES!!

*L*ONG HOURS OF HONEST TOIL BEAR FRUIT AS OUR HEROES BREAK INTO A HUGE UNDERGROUND CAVERN TO BE CONFRONTED BY A *STARTLING* SIGHT!

WE SHOULD BE DIRECTLY *BENEATH* THE WHITE HOUSE NOW...*LENIN'S BEARD!*

BY THE ETERNAL GLACIERS, WHAT *IS* IT?

*A*S FAR AS THE EYE CAN *SEE*, THE RIPPLING MASS STRETCHES OUT INTO THE VERY *DEPTHS* OF THE EARTH!

I'VE *NEVER* SEEN IT'S LIKE! IT'S AN *UNDERGROUND* SEA!

BUT IT'S SURFACE! ...IT DOES *NOT* MOVE LIKE WATER!

THAT'S BECAUSE IT'S *NOT!* COMRADE *AJYS!*

IT'S THE *SOURCE* OF THE CHIEFS POWER..AN ENTIRE OCEAN OF *MONEY*...NO WONDER THESE PEOPLE LIVE IN SUCH *UTTER* POVERTY!

SUCH WEALTH SHOULD *NEVER* BE ACCRUED FOR THE BENEFIT OF ANY *SINGLE* INDIVIDUAL!

FINANCIAL RESOURCES SHOULD *ALWAYS* BE PROPERLY DISTRIBUTED AMONGST THE POPULATION IN AN *EQUAL* FASHION!

HRRRGH!!...THIS IS THE SOURCE OF THE *EVIL*...LET US ...LEAVE THIS PLACE!!

THE STATE *ALONE* SHOULD MANAGE MORTAL RESOURCES IN ACCORDANCE TO THE *GREATER* GOOD!

*S*TEALTHILY, THE FABULOUS FIVE STEP INTO THE *DANK* CORRIDORS THAT EXTEND OUT OF THE CAVERN!

UNNF! WHICH TUNNEL DO WE TAKE?

ONE OF THEM *MUST* LEAD UP INTO THE WHITE HOUSE. WE MAY HAVE TO *SPLIT UP* HERE!

KOMMISSAR, TAKE CARE, I FEAR FOR *YOUR* SAFETY IN THIS SINISTER PLACE!

THANK YOU, COMRADE *AJYS*, BUT YOUR CONCERN SHOULD EXTEND TO *ALL* MEMBERS OF THE GROUP, FOR ALL ARE *EQUALLY* IMPORTANT!

YES...YES OF COURSE YOU ARE *RIGHT*! IF *ONLY* I COULD TELL HIM!

MIG-4 AND I WILL CHECK OUT *THIS* TUNNEL! YOU THREE INVESTIGATE THE *OTHER*. IF YOU FIND *STAVROGIN*, PROCEED TO THE ESCAPE POINT AND STAY IN RADIO CONTACT AT *ALL* TIMES!

..OF COURSE... *KOMMISSAR*... ..GOOD LUCK!

AFTER LONG MINUTES OF SEARCHING, *THE KOMMISSAR* AND *MIG-4* FIND THEMSELVES IN...

..THE *WHITE HOUSE!* WE MUST BE WITHIN IT'S VERY WALLS NOW!

YES, BUT SOMETHING DOES *NOT* FEEL RIGHT! WE MUST BE VIGILANT, YOUNG ONE!

A NEARBY SOUND DRAWS OUR HEROES TO A BALCONY, WHERE THEY WITNESS A *HORRIFYING* SIGHT...

LOOKS LIKE SOMETHING *BIG* IS GOING ON DOWN THERE!

THAT MAN I...I *RECOGNISE* HIM...

FASTER DOLTS, WE MUST GET DER MISSILES TO DER *HIDDEN SILOS* AROUND *RUSSIA*. *IMMEDIATELY! MACH SHNELL!!!*

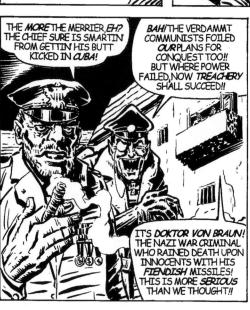

THE *MORE* THE MERRIER, *EH?* THE CHIEF SURE IS SMARTIN' FROM GETTIN' HIS BUTT KICKED IN *CUBA!*

BAH! THE VERDAMMT COMMUNISTS FOILED *OUR* PLANS FOR CONQUEST TOO!! BUT WHERE POWER FAILED, NOW *TREACHERY* SHALL SUCCEED!!

IT'S *DOKTOR VON BRAUN!* THE NAZI WAR CRIMINAL WHO RAINED DEATH UPON INNOCENTS WITH HIS *FIENDISH* MISSILES! THIS IS MORE *SERIOUS* THAN WE THOUGHT!!

MOVING ON, THE DUO ARE DRAWN TO A CERTAIN OFFICE BY AN UNMISTAKABLE, *RANTING* VOICE!

STALIN'S GHOST! ..IT'S...IT'S *HIM!!*

THE MAN HIMSELF! LISTEN, THAT PICTURE OF THE GANGSTER *AL CAPONE* GIVES ME AN IDEA!

WHADDYA' MEAN YA *LOST* 'EM? BUDDY, YOU BETTER HOPE YOUR *INSURANCE* IS PAID UP!!

14

THOSE BUMS, I CAN'T TRUST... *NO!* IT CAN'T BE ...*AL!* IT'S *YOU!* YOU'VE COME BACK!

WHO'D YA THINK IT *WUZ*, YO YO? I HADDA MAKE SURE YOU WUZNT LETTIN THINGS *SLIP!!*

SLIP? NOT ME AL, I WOULDN'T FAIL YA!, YOU WUZ MY *HERO!*

AW *SHADDUP!* LISSEN', WHERE YA KEEPIN THAT *RUSSKIE* BUM?

STAVROGIN? HE'S IN THE *DUNGEON* UNDER THE WEST WING! WE'RE WORKING HIM BUT GOOD, *AL!*

THAT DUMB GORILLA DOESNT REALISE THAT "CAPONE" IS JUST A *PROJECTION* USING MY HEADLIGHTS!..

...AND A LITTLE *VENTRILOQUISM!!*

*A*T THAT PRECISE MOMENT, FATE STEPS IN TO *SHATTER* THE BIZARRE TABLEAU AS...

HERR *CHIEF*, EVERYTHING IS IN READINESS! *GOTT IN HIMMEL!!* VOS IS?

WE'RE *DISCOVERED!!* FLY *MIG-4!* ALERT THE OTHERS!!

ACH! DER FREEDOM COLLECTIVE!!

IT'S A *TRICK!* THEY PLAYED ME LIKE A *RUBE!!* WHY THOSE...

*B*UT BEFORE HE CAN ESCAPE, THE *KOMMISSAR* FINDS HIS ANKLE CAUGHT IN A GRIP OF *STEEL!*

GOT YA!!

YA MADE IT? *GOOD!!* I BIN *ITCHIN* TA GET MY DAINTY PAWS ON YA!!

STRIKE MEIN *PRESIDENT!!!* POUND HIM *MIT YOUR FISTS!!*

I KNEW IT! ...A *TRAP!.*

15

16

..NOT FROM THE *MADMEN!* OR TIN PLATED *GANGSTERS* WHO THINK THEMSELVES ABOVE JUSTICE... WELL THINK *AGAIN* COMRADE!!

NO!..I'M DA CHIEF!! I'M... OOFF!

BAM!

THIS AIN'T HAPPENIN'! THIS AIN'T HAPPENIN'!!

IT'S HAPPENING *CHIEF*, BECAUSE THIS TIME YOU'RE FACING A *FREE MAN!* A *COMMUNIST!!*

AND WE STAND FOR THE FREEDOM OF *ALL* MEN TO *TOIL* FOR THE STATE! SOMETHING YOU CRAVEN CAPITALISTS WILL *NEVER* CRUSH!

GUARDS!! GUARDS!!

AWRIGHT, YA *CORNBALL!* SO YA GOT SOME *FANCY* MOVES ON YA! BUT THAT AIN'T GONNA *PROTECT* YER BUDDIES FROM THE LITTLE *SURPRISE* VON BRAUN WHIPPED UP JUST FOR 'EM!!

TEK!

AT THE TOUCH OF A BUTTON, THE FOUR SINISTER BUSTS SUDDENLY SNAP BACK REVEALING *HIDDEN* SILO'S FROM WHICH LAUNCH...

..MISSILES!!

WELL WHADDYA KNOW THERE AIN'T NO FLIES ON YOU! *HYUK! HYUK!!*

FASTER THAN THE EYE CAN FOLLOW, THE FOUR *MENACING* MISSILES STREAK OFF DOWN THE CORRIDORS TO FIND THEIR *PREY!*

MASTODON

HOMELAND

MIG-L

AND FIND THEY *DO.* EACH ROCKET SPLITS OFF AND PICKS ITS *INDIVIDUAL* TARGET AS THO' POSSESSED BY A MIND OF ITS OWN!

HRRRGH!!.. MASTODON NOT FEAR *PUNY* ROCKET!!

NO *MASTODON!* I SENSE IT CAN HARM *EVEN YOU!*

*E*VEN THE AMAZING *MIG-4* FINDS THAT HE CANNOT OUTDISTANCE THE HURTLING WARHEADS...

I *CAN'T* SHAKE IT, NO MATTER WHAT I DO!!

AN' IT WON'T DO YA NO GOOD TA TRY! *VON BRAUN* RIGGED DEM GIZMO'S TA' HOME IN ON YA *BRAINWAVES!!*

TEEHEEHEE!! *DESTROY* THEM, MY PRETTIES!!

BRAINWAVES, THAT'S THE ANSWER... *MIG-4* LISTEN...

I HEAR YOU, *KOMMISSAR!!.*

*A*T THE KOMMISSAR'S ORDERS, *MIG-4* ALTERS HIS *OWN* ELECTRICAL SYSTEMS TO DUPLICATE THE *BRAINWAVE PATTERNS* OF HIS COMRADES WITH AMAZING RESULTS!!

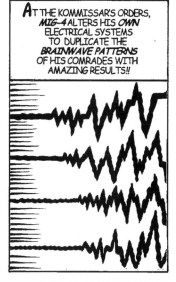

*S*UDDENLY, THE THREE MESSENGERS OF DESTRUCTION VEER *AWAY* FROM THEIR VALIANT TARGETS, TO SEEK *ANOTHER* PREY...

LOOK, THEY'RE *LEAVING!*

*W*ITHIN SECONDS, THE SWARM OF ANNIHILATION IS LOCKED ONTO A *SINGLE* TARGET, JUST A *HAIRSBREADTH* FROM THEIR REACH!

OKAY, I'VE GOT THEM, *KOMMISSAR,* NOW WHAT DO I *DO* WITH THEM?

FOLLOW MY INSTRUCTIONS YOUNG ONE! IT'S TIME THESE MISSILES WERE PUT TO SOME *GOOD!*

18

WHERE IN SAM HILL'S HE TAKIN 'EM?. *OH NO! NO!!*

VAS.. IS?..

TURN 'EM OFF!!..FOR THE LUVVA' PETE! Y'GOTTA TURN 'EM OFF!!

I.. *IMPOSSIBLE!* DER SYSTEMS ARE AUTO LOCKED!

In a *DESPERATE* BURST OF SPEED, *MIG-4* LEADS THE MISSILES INTO THE COLOSSAL CAVERN UNDER THE WHITE HOUSE...

..AND INTO THE *CHIEF'S* OCEAN OF MONEY! A SPLIT SECOND LATER HE EMERGES AS THE WARHEADS *EXPLODE*...

..*S*ETTING *ABLAZE* THE ILL-GOTTEN HOARD! THE WHOLE CAVERN RUMBLES AS GARGANTUAN FLAMES ENGULF *EVERYTHING!!!*

N N N NOOO!!! THE DOUGH!!

*S*IMULTANEOUSLY, *HOMELAND* FINDS HIMSELF SUFFUSED WITH *NEW* ENERGIES!!

THESE ARE THE DUNGEONS. *STAVROGIN* MUST BE HERE!.. HOMELAND! WHAT?

AAAAAAHH!! THIS LAND HAS... BEEN CLEANSED!!

*E*NERGIES WHICH REACH THRU THE VERY SOIL TO *SMASH* INJUSTICE!

HEY! WHA!..

RUN TO THE HILLS! WE CAN JOIN THE *RESISTANCE!*

THOK!

SLAM!

19

WHILE IN THE DUNGEONS BELOW *BORIS STAVROGIN'S* IMPRISONMENT COMES TO AN ABRUPT END...

...NEED REST... MUST SLEEP...

HAW! KEEP WORKIN BUB! IF YOU KNOW WHAT'S *GOOD* FOR YOU AN YOUR FOLKS!

PAPA! IT'S *THE FREEDOM COLLECTIVE!* WE'RE *SAVED!*

LEADING THE FAMILY TO A NEARBY FOREST, THE TRIO REJOIN THE REST OF THE *COLLECTIVE!*

LOOK, THE *RESISTANCE* HAVE MADE A RUNWAY WITH THEIR TORCHES!

ARE YOU SURE YOU *WON'T* COME WITH US?

NO, *KOMMISSAR!* OUR PLACE IS HERE TO CARRY ON THE FIGHT!

MEANWHILE...

CHIEF! WE SPOTTED 'EM GETTIN' INTA' A JET!

FORGET DEM! THE DOUGH'S BOILIN' I'M RUINED!..RUINED!!

..AN IT'S ALL *YOUR* FAULT!!!

N...NEIN *CHIEF!* MY MISSILES VORKED *PERFECTLY!*

TOO PERFECTLY! YA COULDN'T SWITCH 'EM *OFF!!* GUARDS!...GRAB DIS' BUM!!

AS ONE MAN'S NIGHTMARE *BEGINS,* SO DOES ANOTHER'S END!

I WAS SO *WRONG...* I FAILED YOU ALL! I...I DO NOT DESERVE SUCH *LOYALTY* AND *CARE!!*

DO NOT *TORTURE* YOURSELF, COMRADE! THE STATE WILL UNDERSTAND!

CONSIDER YOURSELF FORTUNATE, THAT YOU ALONE WERE GIVEN A *SECOND* CHANCE TO WARN THE PEOPLE OF THE NIGHTMARE THAT IS ...*CAPITALISM!!*

THE END

20

DEDICATED TO *THE MAN* AND *THE KING!*

...I TELL YOU OLD FRIEND, IF ONE MAN WAS PREPARED TO BECOME A *SYMBOL* OF COMMUNISM, EVEN AT THE COST OF HIS *OWN* IDENTITY, HE WOULD BECOME AN INSPIRATION TO A *WORLD* OF WORKERS!

PUFF! PUFF!...BUT *WHERE* WOULD WE FIND SUCH A MAN?

OUT THERE...ON *ANY* STREET CORNER! ANY TRULY LOYAL CITIZEN OF THE STATE WOULD *CERTAINLY* ACCEPT SUCH AN HONOUR!

DETERMINED TO *PROVE* HIS POINT, OUR LEADER AND HIS FRIEND VENTURED OUT INTO THE STREET AND CALLED TO THE *FIRST* MAN THEY MET...

A *MOMENT* OF YOUR TIME, COMRADE...

AFTER LISTENING TO OUR LEADERS DREAMS, THE MAN'S REPLY WAS TO GLADDEN HIS HEART AND *FOREVER* ALTER THE DESTINIES OF FREE MEN!

...THEN I WILL *GLADLY* BE *THAT* MAN COMRADE!

PART OF THE MAN'S TRAINING WAS A PROGRAMME OF *EXERCISES* THE LIKE OF WHICH HAD NEVER BEEN ATTEMPTED BY THOSE OF *LESSER* LOYALTY!

IT WORKS COMRADE LEADER! HE IS DOING THE WORK OF *TWO* OXEN!

WHO THIS MAN WAS WE SHALL NEVER KNOW! WHAT LIFE HE LEFT BEHIND IS NOT IMPORTANT! ALL THAT NEEDS TO BE TOLD IS THAT HE GAVE HIS *ALL* FOR THE STATE...FOR THE *PEOPLE* AS *THE KRIMSON KOMMISSAR!!*

MIG-4'S ORIGIN BEGAN THE DAY THAT MIKHAIL MOLOTOV TOOK AN *UNAUTHORISED* FLIGHT IN THE REVOLUTIONARY *SELF-REPAIRING MIG!*

MOLOTOV, YOU YOUNG HOTHEAD! RETURN TO BASE, THE *MIG* IS TOO *DANGEROUS!!*

THAT IS *WHY* I MUST TEST IT! TO SAVE THE STATE *MORE* LOSSES!

TRAGICALLY, THE YOUNG PILOT *DID* CRASH INTO THE URAL MOUNTAINS, WHERE THE INCREDIBLE MACHINE REPAIRED ITSELF *AROUND* AND *INSIDE* THE BODY OF IT'S STRICKEN PILOT!

TRANSFORMING HIM INTO THE INCREDIBLE *HALF-MAN, HALF-JET PLANE -MIG-4!!*

21

THE WORLDS *STRONGEST* BEAST MAN OWES HIS CREATION TO THE FREAK BLIZZARD THAT SEPARATED MAJOR VLADIMIR VERASHAKIN FROM HIS UNIT DURING ARMY MANOEUVRES IN SIBERIA!

FORCED TO TAKE REFUGE IN A *HIDDEN* CAVE, THE EXHAUSTED SOLDIER MADE A *STARTLING* DISCOVERY....

A *MASTODON!!* FROZEN IN ICE... BUT WHY DOES IT *GLOW* SO?

LITTLE REALISING THAT IT HAD BEEN EXPOSED TO RADIATION FROM RECENT A-BOMB TESTS, VERASHAKIN WAS FORCED TO USE THE BEAST FOR *FOOD*, OBLIVIOUS OF THE *CONSEQUENCES!!*

AND OF THE *FREAK* BIOCHEMICAL REACTION THAT WOULD TRANSFORM HIM INTO THE *MONSTROUS MASTODON!!*

THE ICY WASTES OF SIBERIA ALSO GAVE US THE ICE GODDESS, *AJYS* AND *HOMELAND*, WHO REVEALED THEMSELVES TO THWART CRAVEN YANKEE SABOTEURS!

DIS JOINT IS HAUNTED...*OOFF!!*

BEGONE!! INTRUDERS TO OUR LAND!

RESULTING IN A *HISTORIC* MEETING TAKING PLACE THAT *VERY* DAY!

THEN IT'S *TRUE!* YOU *DO* EXIST!

YES, *GREAT* AND *NOBLE* LEADER!

GODS ARE INDEED *REAL*, BUT MEN DO *NOT* SERVE US, RATHER, IT IS *WE* WHO SERVE MAN AND THE *HIGHEST TRUTH* HE CAN WIELD...*COMMUNISM!!*

AND SO WAS BORN THE LEGENDARY *FREEDOM COLLECTIVE!* GUARDIANS OF *COMMUNISM* AND SWORN ENEMIES OF ALL WHO OPPOSE *STATE SANCTIONED* FREEDOM!!

22

WHAT'S *THIS?* THE WORKERS MOST LOYAL PROTECTORS PITCHED IN POINTLESS *BATTLE* AGAINST ONE ANOTHER.. *HOW* CAN THIS BE? IS IT A *TRICK*, AN IMAGINARY STORY? NO! THIS IS NO *DECADENT* FLIGHT OF FANCY, *THIS* IS STATE SHATTERING REALITY!!

EVER LOYAL *IGOR SLOANO* PRESENTS *THE FREEDOM COLLECTIVE* IN THEIR MOST SENSES SHAKING BATTLE YET, AGAINST THE AWESOME LOYALTY OF *THE SIBERIAN SIX* IN...

"THIS STATE DIVIDED!"

CREDITS:
STATE APPROVED SCRIPT: COMRADE BARR
PROLETARIAT PENCILS AND LETTERING: DOMSKI REGAN
PENCILLING LACKEY: KURT SIBLOMOV
POLITBURO INKS: ALEXSANDER DAVIDOVITCH
UNWAVERING EDITS: IGOR SLOANO

BERLIN. ONCE THE HOME OF THE WOULD-BE WORLD CONQUERING *NAZIS*. NOW A CITY FOREVER SPLIT IN *TWO* FOR THE *GOOD* OF ALL PEOPLE. IT IS HERE THAT OUR *LATEST* DRAMA UNFOLDS.

FOR IT IS HERE THAT LIGHT MET SHADE WITH OUR COURAGEOUS TROOPS *FORCED* INTO AN UNEASY ALLIANCE WITH THE FORCES OF THE WEST TO POLICE THE STREETS OF THE ONCE FASCIST CAPITAL.

NICE DAY, HUH BUB.

JUST KEEP YOUR *HANDS* WHERE I CAN SEE THEM, YANKEE.

BY DAY, ITS CITIZENS WENT ABOUT THEIR TASKS IN AN ATMOSPHERE OF *MISTRUST* IN THIS STRANGE MELTING POT OF FREEDOM AND OPPRESSION.

BUT BY *NIGHT*, ITS OPEN STREETS BECAME AN AVENUE FOR SINISTER NE'R-DO-WELLS TO DELIVER THEIR PACKAGES OF *DESTRUCTION* ACROSS INTO OUR TERRITORY.

NOT *ANOTHER* FACTORY DESTROYED.

THE WORK OF THE WEST NO DOUBT.

AS ALWAYS, THESE *BETRAYALS* DO NOT ESCAPE THE NOTICE OF OUR ESTEEMED LEADER.

THIS IS THE *FOURTH* ACT OF SABOTAGE THIS WEEK LEADER. THE *CHIEF* IS MAKING *FOOLS* OF US ALL.

SIGH! I KNEW THAT NO GOOD WOULD COME OF *TRUSTING* THE WEST OLD FRIEND, EVEN AFTER *SAVING* THEM FROM THE NAZIS.

THOUGH *BURDENED* BY AFFAIRS OF STATE, OUR LEADER STILL FOUND TIME TO READ AND TAKE A *LEAF* FROM HISTORY.

Hmmmmm... IN OLDEN TIMES THEY USED *WALLS* TO KEEP BARBARIANS OUT.

2

AND SO WAS CREATED *THE BERLIN WALL*, THE DIVIDING LINE BETWEEN THE *REASON* OF THE EAST AND THE *MADNESS* OF THE WEST. A MAGNIFICENT EDIFICE THAT WILL STAND FOR A *THOUSAND YEARS* AND MORE.

ALMOST IMMEDIATELY, THE WALL'S PRESENCE WAS FELT.

HUH?!? WHERE'D *THIS* COME FROM?

I DUNNO' BUT WE GOTTA' DRAW STRAWS TO SEE WHO GETS TO *TELL* THE CHIEF!

INEVITABLY, WORD OF THE REMARKABLE STRUCTURE REACHED THE *EARS* OF THE MISTER BIG OF INTERNATIONAL CAPITALISM, WHO WAS ALSO WELL READ... IN HIS *OWN* FASHION.

ER...CHIEF, THERE'S SOMETHING I GOTTA TELL YA...

SHADDAP! I *ALREADY* KNOW. BUT THIS BOOK OF VON BRAUN'S HAS JUST GIVEN ME AN *IDEA*.

BUT NOW WE MOVE FORWARD IN TIME TO THE PRESENT, WHERE A STARTLING SIGHT CAN BE WITNESSED TAKING PLACE AT THAT SELFSAME WALL.

DOWN WIT' THE *WEST*. WE WANT *WAR*!

YEAH... *BURN* 'EM ALL DOWN!

LOOK OUT-GLUMPH!

HEY... WHA-

YOU DUMB YANKEES ARE TOO *SLOW*. WE'RE GONNA' RUN RINGS ROUND YA'... LIKE SO. AINT' THAT RIGHT *MIG-4*?

OR *FLY* 'EM KOMMISSAR. HAR HAR!

RAHHH!!.. MASTODON *CRUSH* YA ALL!

LOOK OUT. HE'S-

OUCH, HEY!

DUNK

3

BUT NOW OUR FOCUS MUST DRAW AWAY FROM THESE FIVE FOOLS TO A SCIENTIFIC LABOR CAMP ON THE DARKER SIDE OF THE WALL, WHERE ANOTHER OF THE CHIEF'S SINISTER PLANS IS UNDERWAY.

HERE'S ALLA' THE *CAPTIVE* EGGHEADS LIKE YA' ORDERED CHIEF.

WOTTA' BUNCH OF *LOSERS*. YOU! WORD IS, YOU'RE THE *SMARTEST* OUTTA' THESE BOZOS. LISSEN UP, I GOT A *TASK* FER YA.

NO MORE PLEASE. SINCE YOU *FAKED* MY DEATH AND *ABDUCTED* ME, I'VE DONE NOTHING BUT MAKE WEAPONS FOR YOU.

AN' YOU'RE GONNA' WHIP ME A DOOZY *THIS* TIME. I WANT THIS BABY UP AN' RUNNIN' BY THIS AFTERNOON OR IT'S THE *MINES* FOR THE LOTTA' YA!

YA REALLY THINK THIS THING'S GONNA' TAKE OUT THE *BERLIN WALL*, CHIEF?

IT *BETTER*. IF I DON'T GET ME THAT RUSSKIE LOOT I'M *SUNK*. THE *COLLECTIVE* BURNED ME BUT *GOOD* LAST TIME WE TUSSLED WITH THEM BUMS.

ONCE THOSE *PATSIES* IN BERLIN HAVE GIVEN ME THE EXCUSE TA *INVADE* THE COMMIES, I'LL HAVE ALL THEIR *RICHES* FOR MYSELF.

I'LL BE ABLE TO FUND MY PROGRAM FOR THE *CONQUEST OF SPACE*. NO ONE WILL BE ABLE TO STOP ME.

I'LL EXPAND MY GRASP TA HAUL IN THE DOUGH FROM *OTHER PLANETS*. I'LL HAVE A BANK BALANCE LIKE NO-ONE'S EVER SEEN.

B-BUT CHIEF, AIN'T THE *FREEDOM COLLECTIVE* GONNA' TRY TO STOP YA?

DON'T WORRY ABOUT THOSE YO-YO'S. I GOTTA' *TRICK* OR TWO UP MY SLEEVE TA HANDLE THEM. ACSHULLY, I GOT *SIX*. HUR HUR!!!

5

WE SHIFT OUR ATTENTION ONCE MORE FROM THE MACHINATIONS OF A *MADMAN* TO A PARTICULAR STATUE IN THE BRIGHT CITY OF *LENINGRAD*.

BUT THIS IS NO *ORDINARY* STATUE. INSIDE IS THE MINIATURIZED HEADQUARTERS OF THE *SIBERIAN SIX* WHERE WE FIND THE GROUP'S LEADER *PROFESSOR SIX* RECEIVING A MESSAGE OF GRIM IMPORT.

I SEE. IT'S INCREDIBLE... BUT I UNDERSTAND. I KNOW WHAT *MUST* BE DONE.

WHAT IS IT RUDOLPH?

TROUBLE OLGA, *BIG* TROUBLE. ALERT THE OTHERS IMMEDIATELY.

ELSEWHERE WITHIN THE AMAZING INSTALLATION WE FIND *THE TRACTOR* AND *THE SONIC SOVIET* ENGAGED IN A WASTEFUL ARGUMENT.

LISTEN YOU CUT-RATE FOG HORN, ONE MORE JOKE ABOUT MY *TRACKS* AND I'LL—

YEAH, YOU AND WHAT *ARMY* COMRADE?

THAT'S *ENOUGH*, BOTH OF YOU.

BICKERING LIKE A COUPLE OF *AMERICANS*. DESIST, OR I'LL TURN BOTH OF YOU INTO *WOOD* FOR AN HOUR, UNDERSTOOD?

COMRADES, IT'S A *RED ALERT*. LETS GO.

WERE ANYONE TO GLANCE UP AT THIS STATUE AT THIS VERY MOMENT, THEY WOULD PERHAPS DISCERN A *TINY* FLYING SPECK, NOT UNLIKE AN *INSECT*, HURTLING UPWARDS FROM A HIDDEN LAUNCH BAY WITHIN ITS ARM.

AN OBJECT THAT *INCREASES* RAPIDLY IN SIZE TO BECOME THE AWESOME *SIX CARRIER*.

WHAT IS OUR MISSION COMRADE?

INCREDIBLE AS IT MAY SEEM, THE *FREEDOM COLLECTIVE* ARE ACTING *WITHOUT* STATE SANCTION. WE'VE BEEN ORDERED TO BRING THEM IN FOR *QUESTIONING*.

RUDOLPH, I'VE *LOCATED* THEM JUST 200 KM NORTH OF MOGILEV.

BUT NOW IT IS TIME FOR OUR HEROES TO MAKE THEIR BELATED APPEARANCE IN THIS DRAMA. SO, AT A SABOTAGE RIDDEN FACTORY IN THAT SELF-SAME AREA...

IT LOOKS LIKE *BOTH* YOUR SENIOR CRAFTSMEN WERE ALSO INVOLVED. I'M AFRAID WE MUST NOW INTERROGATE ALL MEMBERS OF YOUR WORKFORCE, *INCLUDING* THEIR FAMILIES FOR—

KOMMISSAR, LOOK!

THE SIBERIAN SIX. WHAT'S GOING ON HERE?

DON'T ACT *INNOCENT* COMRADE. WE'RE HERE TO ARREST YOU *ALL* FOR SUBVERSIVE BEHAVIOR.

IS THIS A *JOKE*, COMRADE? THE COLLECTIVE WOULD *NEVER* ACT AGAINST STATE INTERESTS.

THAT'S FOR *US* TO DETERMINE KOMMISSAR. NOW COME QUIETLY.

ALAS, IT IS OFTEN THE MOST LOYAL WHO CAN REACT WITH *RASHNESS*. WITNESS THE DIM MIND OF *MASTODON* AS HE TRIES TO COMPREHEND THIS *TERRIBLE* ACCUSATION.

VERY WELL COMRADE, LETS GET TO THE *BOTTOM* OF THIS.

THEY SAY... MASTODON... *BETRAY* STATE?!!

RAAAAHHH!! MASTODON *NEVER* BETRAY THE STATE. MASTODON *SMASH* LITTLE MAN.

MASTODON! NO!

LOOK OUT, THEY'RE *GOING* TO—

HRRAAAH! MASTODON SMASH METAL MAN!

ALTHOUGH IT'S *COUNTER-PRODUCTIVE*, I'VE ALWAYS WANTED TO TEST MY *HYDRAULICS* AGAINST YOUR BRUTE STRENGTH.

NOW HOLD *STILL* WHILE I TURN YOU INTO NEXT YEAR'S LANDFILL.

7

YOU HAVE... COURAGE AND LOYALTY LITTLE ONE... BUT SOMETIMES... THEY ARE *NOT* ENOUGH.

OHHHH! LET ME GO, YOU BIG LUMP OF ROCK.

FINALLY, *BOREALIS GIRL* LASHES OUT WITH HER AWESOME ENERGIES, SMASHING THE STARTLED SPIRIT OF THE SOIL INTO A *THOUSAND* PIECES.

FORGIVE ME COMRADE HOMELAND, BUT I CANNOT STAND BY WHILE YOU *BULLY* ONE OF MY TEAM-MATES.

SSHZZAKK!

WITH CLARITY BORN OF *SELFLESS* DEDICATION, THE KOMMISSAR OFFERS A *SOLUTION* TO THE CONFLICT.

PROFESSOR SIX, THIS IS POINTLESS. WE'RE TOO *EVENLY* MATCHED. I SUBMIT FOR FULL TELEPATHIC INTERROGATION IMMEDIATELY.

YOU KNOW WHAT THIS *MEANS*? VERY WELL, PREPARE YOURSELF.

THE BATTLEGROUND FALLS SILENT AND THE COMBATANTS STARE IN AWE AS THE KOMMISSAR AND THE PROFESSOR PREPARE FOR THE *STATE SANCTIONED* TELEPATHIC INTERROGATION.

SLOWLY, THE MOST POWERFUL COMMUNIST TELEPATH ON EARTH REACHES *DEEP* INTO THE KOMMISSAR'S MIND TO UNCOVER THE *TRUTH*.

AND FINDS ONLY *LOYALTY*... SELFLESS, DEVOTED LOYALTY TO THE HIGHER TRUTH OF THE WILL OF THE STATE.

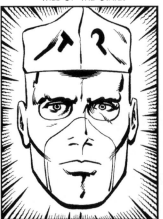

LOYALTY SO *PURE* THAT EVEN THE DEDICATED PROFESSOR IS STAGGERED BY ITS INTENSITY.

I... I HAD NO IDEA. YOUR LOYALTY IS *BEYOND* QUESTION. WE HAVE BEEN *DECEIVED*. FORGIVE ME KOMMISSAR.

THERE IS *NOTHING* TO FORGIVE COMRADE.

YOU PLACED CONCERNS OF THE STATE *ABOVE* PERSONAL LOYALTY. SUCH ACTIONS ARE TO BE *COMMENDED*.

KOMMISSAR!

WE'VE JUST RECEIVED A REPORT THAT THE COLLECTIVE ARE AT THIS MOMENT *ATTACKING* AMERICAN BORDER GUARDS AT THE BERLIN WALL. IT'S IMPOSSIBLE.

Hmmmmm... I SUSPECT THE *ANSWER* TO THIS MYSTERY LIES THERE, PROFESSOR.

THE KOMMISSAR'S *UNQUESTIONABLE* WISDOM ONCE AGAIN PROVES SOUND AS THIS GRIM TABLEAUX CONTINUES IN THE CITY OF FALLEN TYRANTS.

HAW! LOOKIT' THE DUMB YANKEES!

YOU AIN'T GETTIN' AWAY WIT' THIS. WAIT TILL THE *CHIEF* FINDS OUT.

GOING SOMEWHERE COMRADES?

ULP... THE *FREEDOM COLLECTIVE!*

AND THE *SIBERIAN SIX!*

10

A SHORT EXCHANGE LATER...

..SO THAT WUZ THE *PLAN*. WE HADDA' RAISE SOME RUCKUS SO'S THE CHIEF COULD *INVADE* AN' GRAB ALL YER *RICHES* FOR HISSELF. IT WUZN'T OUR IDEA. ME AND THE BOYS HERE ARE JUST CARNY PERFORMERS.

RICHES?

SURELY, THEY MUST RECOGNIZE THAT THE *TRUE* WEALTH OF ANY NATION LIES NOT IN GAUDY BAUBLES OR DECADENT MATERIALISTIC COMFORTS BUT IN THE UNQUESTIONING *DEDICATION* OF ITS CITIZENS?

WELL SAID YOUNG ONE. ALAS THESE ARE RICHES THAT CANNOT BE RECOGNIZED BY A NATION THAT HAS *NEVER* POSSESSED THEM.

KOMMISSAR... MY RADIO!

THE CHIEF! WE'VE PLAYED RIGHT INTO HIS HANDS.

...ICH BIN EIN BERLINER...

...WHO AIN'T ABOUT TA TAKE THIS LATEST *PROVOCATION* LAYIN' DOWN. WE BIN PREPARIN' A LITTLE SURPRISE TA DEAL WITH THE *COMMIE MENACE* IN BERLIN. SHE OUGHTTA' BE COMIN' YER WAY *RIGHT* ABOUT NOW!

KOMMISSAR... WHAT DOES HE MEAN?

I DON'T KNOW. WAIT... WHAT'S THAT NOISE?

THOOM! THOOM! THOOM!

THE GROUND... IT'S SHAKING. IT SOUNDS LIKE *FOOTSTEPS*.

BY ALL THAT'S LOYAL!!

THOOM! THOOM! THOOM!

IT'S IMPOSSIBLE... IT *CAN'T* BE!

THOOM! THOOM! THOOM!

BUT IT IS!!

11

JOLLY JACK TARR

FIRST APPEARED IN
F.C. #17 SEPT.

ANY DEDICATED DEFENDER OF THE STATE WHO TACKLES THIS BRITISH BAD GUY IS LIABLE TO FIND THEMSELVES IN A STICKY SITUATION! ABLE TO TRANSFORM HIS BODY INTO A MASS OF SENTIENT, STATE-THREATENING **TAR**, JOLLY JACK HAS DRIPPED AND OOZED HIS WAY INTO BECOMING ONE OF THE COLLECTIVE'S MOST DANGEROUS ENEMIES! HIS MENACE HAS DOUBLED RECENTLY DUE TO HIS JOINING THE NOTORIOUS **BRITANNIA BATTALION!**

PART 2

"WHERE MONUMENTS DWELL!"

INCREDIBLE... THEY'VE *MECHANIZED* ONE OF THEIR MONUMENTS!

STAND BACK COMRADES. THAT OVERGROWN PAPERWEIGHT MEANS *TROUBLE!*

IT'S *MONSTROUS!* WE HAVE TO KEEP IT AWAY FROM THE WALL!

IT... TAINTS THE SOIL... WITH ITS *THREAT...*

WITHOUT A WORD, THE *AWESOME AUTOMATA* RAISES ITS TITANIC TORCH LIKE A MONSTROUS WAR-CLUB.

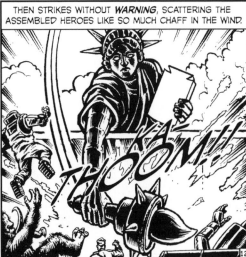

THEN STRIKES WITHOUT *WARNING*, SCATTERING THE ASSEMBLED HEROES LIKE SO MUCH CHAFF IN THE WIND.

KATHOOM!!!

12

WITHOUT THOUGHT FOR PERSONAL SAFETY, THE GREATEST ASSEMBLY OF SUPER-COMMUNISTS EVER, HURL THEMSELVES INTO THE FRAY TO PROTECT A MONUMENT OF FREEDOM AGAINST ONE OF OPPRESSION.

AND YET EVEN THIS NOBLE ATTEMPT IS SWEPT ASIDE BY *CORRUPT* POWER BEYOND MEASURE.

EVEN MY WOODEN TOUCH HAS NO EFFECT. IT'S LIKE IT'S RECEIVING POWER FROM AN *OUTSIDE* SOURCE.

INDUCTION, IT'S THE *ONLY* ANSWER!

INDUCTION?

OUR RESEARCHERS ARE WORKING ON A METHOD OF BROADCASTING NOT ONLY SIGNALS, BUT *POWER ITSELF* TO A SPECIALLY ATTUNED RECEIVER. IN THIS WAY, ANY OBJECT COULD BE IMBUED WITH *LIMITLESS* POWER.

ONLY *ONE* MAN IN THE WEST HAD THE BRILLIANCE TO RIVAL *STATE SCIENTISTS* IN THIS FIELD, BUT HE IS NO LONGER WITH US... STRANGE.

RUDOLF, I HAVE A SUGGESTION.

I... I THINK I MAY BE ABLE TO ATTUNE MY ENERGY WIELDING ABILITY TO *BLOCK* THE ROBOTS POWER FLOW.

Hmmmm! IT'S *INCREDIBLY RISKY* MY LOYAL WIFE, BUT FOR THE GOOD OF THE STATE, I AUTHORIZE YOU TO TRY IT. 13

THE BRAVE BOREALIS GIRL ATTEMPTS THE DARING FEAT. HOWEVER THE RESULTS ARE **NOT** AS EXPECTED AS SHE FINDS BOTH HERSELF AND THE KOMMISSAR TRANSFORMING INTO PURE ENERGY.

YES, I'VE FOUND THE **FREQUENCY**... I... OOOOOHHH!!

BOREALIS GIRL!

INSTANTLY THE TWO HEROES FIND THEMSELVES DRAWN ALONG TO THE **SOURCE** OF THE ROBOTS ENERGY BROADCAST.

WHAT HAS HAPPENED?

MY... MY POWERS HAVE **CHANGED** RECENTLY*. I'VE FOUND THAT I AM NOW ABLE TO TRANSFORM MATTER INTO ENERGY. I... I WAS INTENDING TO INFORM THE STATE OF THIS CHANGE BUT WE HAVE BEEN BUSY BATTLING RASPUTIN AND THE SILVER SENATOR.

*SEE SS #14. SMILING SLOANO!

WITHIN MERE MOMENTS, THE TWO MATERIALIZE DEEP **BEHIND** ENEMY LINES.

HMMM, I SEE... WE WILL DISCUSS THIS **LATER**. WE SEEM TO HAVE ARRIVED AT THE **SOURCE** OF THE ENERGY.

LOOK, **CAPTIVE** SCIENTISTS SENDING POWER TO THE ROBOT!

NOT FOR MUCH LONGER BOREALIS GIRL. ON MY COMMAND...

SOON... HOW CAN WE THANK YOU?

YOUR FREEDOM WILL BE **REWARD** ENOUGH, COMRADE.

YOU MUST GET AWAY!

YOU!... SO YOUR DEATH WAS **FALSE**. WE CANNOT LEAVE UNTIL WE HAVE **DEACTIVATED** YOUR ROBOTS POWER SOURCE.

BUT, YOU DO NOT UNDERSTAND, I DID NOT MAKE JUST **ONE**—

KOMMISSAR! LOOK OUT!!

I FIGGERED YA BUMS MIGHT TRY STICKIN' YER NOSES IN, SO I HAD THE EGGHEADS COOK UP **KNUCKLES** HERE TA GIVE YA ALL A **WARM** WELCOME.

14

WHILE BACK IN BERLIN, ANOTHER UNEQUAL BATTLE RAGES. WITH THE MONSTROUS POWER OF ONE OPPONENT MATCHED ONLY BY THE VALIANT DETERMINATION OF THE OTHER.

IT'S NO USE... WE ARE ONLY SLOWING IT DOWN.

I'M AFRAID WE'VE GOT OTHER PROBLEMS NOW COMRADES.

AND WHAT HAS MIG-4 SEEN? NO LESS THAN THE MARCHING HORDES OF CAPITALISM NOW EMBOLDENED TO LAUNCH THEIR ASSAULT ON OUR NATIONS.

BUT NOW THE FIGHT TAKES AN EVEN MORE SINISTER TURN AS THE MONSTROUS MECHANOID STOPS IN ITS TRACKS AND AIMS ITS TORCH AT OUR HEROES.

THE TORCH, IT'S GLOWING.

I WAS AFRAID OF THIS. IT'S SOME KIND OF ENERGY WEAPON.

UNFLINCHING, THE ASSEMBLED DEFENDERS OF THE STATE STAND THEIR GROUND, BRACING THEMSELVES FOR THE DEVASTATING RELEASE OF THE GARGANTUA'S ENERGIES.

SSSSSSIZZZZZ!

MEANWHILE...

DAT'S WHAT I LIKE ABOUT YOU REDS... YER JUST TOO STUPID TA KNOW WHEN YER BEATEN. IT JUST MEANS THAT I CAN GIVE YA THE OLD ONE TWO AGAIN!

HEY! YA AIN'T WIMPIN' OUT ON ME, ARE YA? I WANT A COUPLE MORE ROUNDS. YA HEAR ME?

I HEAR YOU, CHIEF. NOW YOU HEAR ME...

16

YOU LAUGH AT OUR WAY OF *LIFE*. YOU CALL US *WEAK*. YOU THINK OUR LOYALTY *STUPID*...

WELL, THE NAZIS WEREN'T LAUGHING AS IT *CRUSHED* THEM. THEY COULDN'T WIN AND *NEITHER* WILL YOU...

BECAUSE I'M *NOT* IMPORTANT, ALL THAT MATTERS IS OBEYING THE WILL OF THE STATE WITHOUT QUESTION, *EVEN* IF IT MEANS YOUR DEATH... IS *THAT* STUPID MR. PRESIDENT?

WHA?

..AND CAN A STUPID MAN KNOW THAT IT IS POSSIBLE TO TRIGGER AN *OVERLOAD* BY FUSING THESE TWO TERMINALS LIKE *THIS*?

HEY! WHADDYA' DOIN' UP THERE? *STOP*... NO. NO!!

WITH A THUNDEROUS EXPLOSION THE HULKING IRONCLAD IS REDUCED TO A MASS OF *CRACKLING* FRAGMENTS...

SSSHHRRAAK!

AS ITS UNLEASHED ENERGIES SURGE *BACK* INTO THE AGONIZED FORM OF ITS DESPOTIC CONTROLLER.

ENERGIES SO *VAST*, THEY CAN NO LONGER BE *CONTAINED* BY MERE TECHNOLOGY, AND SO BURST FORTH TO *CONSUME* EVERYTHING IN THEIR PATH.

17

NO TIME TO WASTE, BOREALIS GIRL. OUR COMRADES AT THE *WALL* NEED OUR HELP. WE MUST DEACTIVATE THE GENERATOR *NOW*.

LET ME HELP YOU... PLEASE.

VERY WELL... I SENSE THAT YOU DID *NOT* SERVE THE CAPITALISTS WILLINGLY.

IT'S TRUE, I WAS *FORCED*. BUT I WAS WEAK... WE *ALL* WERE.

WE *ALLOW* YOUR TYRANNY TO RULE OUR LIVES... I *LET* YOU FORCE ME TO CREATE YOUR ENGINES OF DEVASTATION. IT TOOK THESE COMMUNISTS TO SHOW ME THAT YOU *CAN* BE FOUGHT. BECAUSE OF THEM I'M *FREE* NOW.

REST EASY, COMRADE! THE POWER YOU UNLEASHED WILL BE IN THE HANDS OF *STATE SCIENTISTS* WHO WILL WIELD IT FOR THE *GOOD* OF ALL PEOPLE!

THANK THE STATE. BUT NOW, LET US THWART THE *REST* OF THAT TYRANT'S PLAN.

I CAN *DRAIN* THE ROBOTS POWER FROM HERE WHILE THE CARRIER WAVE WILL *RETURN* YOU AND THE OTHERS TO FREEDOM. ARE YOU READY?

AS READY AS I'LL EVER BE.

THEN GOOD LUCK. ONCE YOU'RE ALL AWAY, I'LL *DESTROY* THE GENERATORS AS YOU SAID.

THANK YOU.

NO, THANK *YOU* KOMMISSAR.

ELSEWHERE AT THE BASE, THE TYRANT'S LACKEYS MAKE A *DISCOVERY* AMIDST THE RUBBLE.

IT'S THE CHIEF. HE'S *ALIVE*, BUT BARELY. WE GOTTA' GET HIM TA SAFETY!

WHY?

CUZ HE AINT' *PAID* US DUM DUM!

IN THE BLINK OF AN EYE, THE KOMMISSAR AND THE OTHERS FIND THEMSELVES *BACK* IN BERLIN.

KOMMISSAR. YOU'RE SAFE... THANK THE STATE!

GOOD TO HAVE YOU BACK COMRADES.

NO TIME FOR IDLE BANTER. HOW FARES THE BATTLE?

IT'S WEAPON BLINKED OUT A SECOND AGO. IT SEEMS TO BE GETTING *WEAKER*!

AYE, AND ITS STENCH EBBS BY THE MINUTE.

A SHAME THE SAME CANNOT BE SAID ABOUT THE CHIEF'S TROOPS. I *CANNOT* HOLD THE WALL MUCH LONGER!

...THE STRAIN... IS TOO GREAT... THEIR *GREED* HAS... DRIVEN THEM INSANE...

INEXORABLY, THE GARGANTUAN PRESSURE MOUNTS AS THE GRASPING HORDES FIGHT TOOTH AND NAIL TO BREACH THE WALL TWIXT' THE *CIVILIZED* WORLD AND THEIRS.

SIR! I JUS' GOT THE WORD, THE CHIEF'S BEEN LAID OUT *AGAIN*!

BIG DEAL, I NEVER LIKED DA' BUM ANYWAY. IT JUST MEANS THERE'S *MORE* FOR US... FORWARD?!!

AS THE FIRST CRACKS APPEAR IN THE *NOBLE* EDIFICE, THE PEOPLE'S HEROES STAND FIRM IN THEIR DARKEST HOUR.

COULD THIS BE THE *END*? IF SO, LET ME FACE IT AT YOUR *SIDE* MY KOMMISSAR.

DO NOT DESPAIR COMRADE AJYS. I HAVE *PLANNED* FOR THIS MOMENT. AWAIT MY SIGNAL ALL OF YOU AND STRIKE TOGETHER AS *ONE*!

THAT'S THE CHIEF *AWAY.* WE GOTTA' SECURE THE REST OF THE... HEY! *WHO'S* THAT AT THE GENERATORS?

I?... MERELY ONE WHO SERVED YOU IN LIFE...

...WHO SLAVED FOR YOUR WARMONGERING CAPITALIST EMPIRE. BUT NO *LONGER.* NOW I DIE A FREE MAN, A *COMMUNIST!*

DON'T TRIGGER THAT SWITCH, YA BUM!

A THROWN SWITCH... A SIMPLE HUMAN GESTURE. BUT ONE THAT HAS REPERCUSSIONS MILES DISTANT WHERE ORDER CLASHES WITH CHAOS.

THAT FLASH... WHAT?

IT'S THE *SIGNAL!* EVERYONE STRIKE NOW!!

GENERATIONS UNBORN WILL SPEAK OF THE MOMENT WHEN THE COMBINED POWER OF FREEDOM WAS UNLEASHED TO FOREVER CRUSH THIS *DARKEST* OF ALL MENACES!

THOOM!

WITH A SCREECH OF COLLAPSING METAL, THE SINISTER SYMBOL TOPPLES *BACK* INTO ITS OWN DECADENT DOMAIN, *BURYING* THE GRASPING HORDES ONCE AND FOR ALL.

KKKRREEASSH!

THAT'S THE *LAST* OF THEM. THE WALL IS SAFE. WHEW! KOMMISSAR, WHAT A SIGHT!

A *GLORIOUS* SIGHT YOUNG ONE...SO LONG AS IT IS FOR THE PROTECTION OF THE STATE AND THE PEOPLE!

NOW BACK TO CIVILIZATION. I HAVE SOME QUESTIONS FOR BOREALIS GIRL.

20

THE END!

PROFESSOR SIX AND THE ORIGIN OF THE SIBERIAN SIX!

AS EVERYONE KNOWS, I LED A TEAM OF SCIENTIFIC ADVENTURERS INTO THE UNKNOWN WILDS OF THE TUNGUSKA REGION OF SIBERIA TO UNCOVER THE CAUSE OF THE MYSTERIOUS EXPLOSION OF 1908.

AND FIND WE DID. BUT NOT EVEN WE COULD HAVE BEEN PREPARED FOR THE AWESOME CONSEQUENCES OF OUR BEING EXPOSED TO COSMIC ENERGIES STORED WITHIN THE METEOR.

ENERGIES THAT IMBUED MY FELLOW PROFESSORS, STUDENTS AND GUIDE WITH ABILITIES FAR BEYOND THOSE OF MORTAL MAN.

RUDOLPH RUDENKO: PROFESSOR SIX.

OLGA RUDENKO: BOREALIS GIRL.

GREGOR MAKALOV: THE WOODEN GARGOYLE.

OSKAR ORLOVA: THE SONIC SOVIET.

TATIANA ORLOVA: MAGNET GIRL.

BORIS BULGARIN: THE TRACTOR.

REALIZING THAT WITH GREAT POWER COMES GREAT RESPONSIBILITY TO THE STATE, WE PLEDGED AT THAT MOMENT TO USE NEW-FOUND ABILITIES FOR ITS UNQUESTIONING PROTECTION. FROM THIS WAS BORN THE AWESOME **SIBERIAN SIX!**

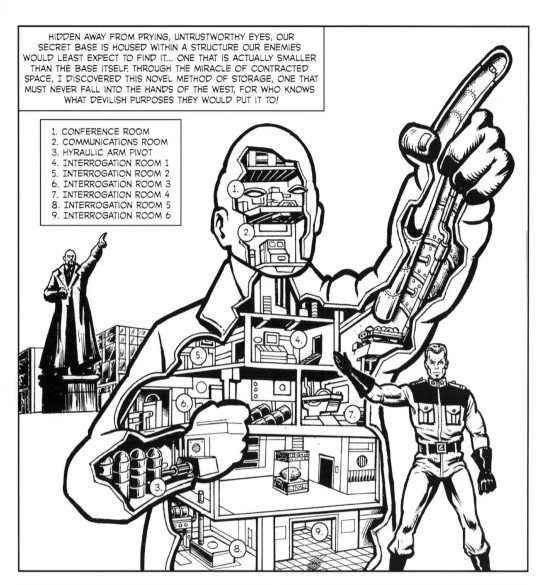

HIDDEN AWAY FROM PRYING, UNTRUSTWORTHY EYES, OUR SECRET BASE IS HOUSED WITHIN A STRUCTURE OUR ENEMIES WOULD LEAST EXPECT TO FIND IT... ONE THAT IS ACTUALLY SMALLER THAN THE BASE ITSELF. THROUGH THE MIRACLE OF CONTRACTED SPACE, I DISCOVERED THIS NOVEL METHOD OF STORAGE, ONE THAT MUST NEVER FALL INTO THE HANDS OF THE WEST, FOR WHO KNOWS WHAT DEVILISH PURPOSES THEY WOULD PUT IT TO!

1. CONFERENCE ROOM
2. COMMUNICATIONS ROOM
3. HYRAULIC ARM PIVOT
4. INTERROGATION ROOM 1
5. INTERROGATION ROOM 2
6. INTERROGATION ROOM 3
7. INTERROGATION ROOM 4
8. INTERROGATION ROOM 5
9. INTERROGATION ROOM 6

OF SPECIAL INTEREST TO OUR YOUNG READERS ARE OUR COSTUMES WHICH ARE ABLE TO ADAPT TO OUR INDIVIDUAL POWERS. THIS IS DUE TO THEIR BEING COMPOSED OF AGITATED ATOMS. THESE LOYAL PARTICLES HAVE BEEN LIBERATED FROM THE TYRANNY OF NORMAL MATTER AND NOW FOLLOW STATE-APPROVED PATHS IN RESPONSE TO WHATEVER SUPERPOWER THEY COME IN CONTACT WITH.

AND LASTLY, THE AWESOME METEOR THAT GAVE US OUR POWERS, AND FROM WHICH WE MUST RECHARGE PERIODICALLY. FROM WHENCE IT CAME AND AS TO ITS TRUE NATURE, THAT STILL REMAINS A MYSTERY. ALTHOUGH MY RECENT RESEARCH INDICATES THAT IT IS ARTIFICIAL. PERHAPS A GIFT BY COMMUNISTS FROM SPACE... ONLY TIME WILL TELL!

22

DEEP WITHIN THE KREMLIN, WITHIN THE VERY WALLS OF K.R.U.S.H (KREMLIN RESPONSE UNIT, SUPREME HEADQUARTERS) A GRIM TABLEAU UNFOLDS...

THESE TWO ATOMIC POWER STATIONS WERE **ATTACKED** LAST NIGHT. THAT MAKES **FIVE** IN THE LAST TWO WEEKS.

FOR IT IS HERE THAT IVAN KARNAGE, DIRECTOR OF K.R.U.S.H., CONFERS WITH ANOTHER LOYAL SERVANT OF THE STATE, THE KRIMSON KOMMISSAR: POLITICAL OFFICER OF THE FREEDOM COLLECTIVE.

IN EACH CASE THE ATTACK IS IDENTICAL, THE STATIONS ARE ALL STRUCK FROM **BENEATH** THE GROUND.

AND YOU SUSPECT THE **AMERICANS?**

THEM...OR SOMETHING **EQUALLY** AS SINISTER. THIS IMAGE WAS CAUGHT BY SECURITY CAMERA JUST BEFORE THE LATEST ATTACK. HAVE YOU EVER SEEN ITS LIKE?

IT...IT LOOKS LIKE THE PERISCOPE OF A **SUBMARINE**. BUT THAT'S IMPOSSIBLE, THAT GROUND'S SOLID CONCRETE.

WE'VE GOT TO GET TO THE BOTTOM OF IT COMRADE! ITS BAD ENOUGH HAVING TO DEAL WITH SUBVERSION AND BETRAYAL ON OUR OWN SOIL, NOW TO BE ATTACKED FROM BENEATH IT...

HMMMM...IT COULD BE THE WORK OF THE **SUBTERRANEAN SENATOR,** ALTHOUGH IT'S NOT HIS USUAL STYLE!

RED ALERT! RED ALERT! THE DUBYINKO ATOMIC POWER STATION IS UNDER ATTACK FROM AN UNKNOWN SOURCE!!

THE ALARM!

WELL COMRADE, IT LOOKS AS THOUGH WE MAY FACE OUR UNKNOWN FOE **SOONER** THAN WE HAD ANTICIPATED!

AND SO OUR FEARLESS, STATE SERVING, HEROES RACE TO CONFRONT THEIR SINISTER ADVERSARY...

THE **HELIJET** WILL GET US THERE IN MINUTES!

YES, BUT TO FACE **WHAT?**

1

IT'S **SUBMERGING**! I SWEAR THOSE JOKERS BACK AT K.R.U.S.H. MUST HAVE SPIKED MY VODKA!

CALM YOURSELF COMRADE. THERE MUST BE A RATIONAL EXPLANATION...A **SCIENTIFIC** ONE!

BUT NOW WE CAST OUR EYES BACK TO K.R.U.S.H. HEADQUARTERS AND THE S.D.U.* DIVISION WHERE THE **AMAZING** HUMANOID RECORDERS ARE CREATED TO PROTECT US FROM SUBVERSION **WITHIN** OUR OWN RANKS...AND EVEN OUR **FAMILIES**...

THAT-IS-INTERESTING-COMRADE-TELL-ME-MORE.

THAT-IS-INTERESTING-GRANDFATHER-TELL-ME-MORE.

*SUBVERSION DETECTOR UNITS...EVER WATCHFUL IGOR.

EVEN HERE, WORD OF THE AMAZING APPARITION REACHES THE EARS OF **ASTONISHED** SCIENTISTS AND TECHNICIANS.

INCREDIBLE!

IT'S...IT'S UNCANNY!

BUT THERE IS **ONE** FOR WHOM THE APPEARANCE OF THE SINISTER SUBMERSIBLE REAWAKENS THE COLD DREAD OF A NIGHTMARE BELIEVED LONG FORGOTTEN!

IT'S **THEM**!...THEY'VE RETURNED AFTER **ALL** THESE YEARS!

AND SO, A SHORT WHILE LATER IN KARNAGE'S OFFICE...

DON'T HAND ME THAT SUPERSTITIOUS DRIVEL COMRADE! THAT SUB IS AS **REAL** AS YOU OR I...AND IF IT'S REAL THEN IT'S DETECTABLE! SO GET TO IT...OR DO I HAVE TO COME DOWN THERE **PERSONALLY**?

I DON'T UNDERSTAND HOW THEY ACHIEVED THIS. NAZI TECHNOLOGY WAS ALWAYS **FAR** BEHIND OURS!

THE ANSWER IS SIMPLE COMRADE! THEY DID NOT INVENT IT...THEY **STOLE** IT!

WAIT! I **RECOGNISE** HIM!

3

PROFESSOR KEREZOVA OF THE **RESEARCH** DIVISION!

IF YOU KNOW SOMETHING THEN YOU'D BETTER **TELL** US COMRADE!

"...IT WAS DURING **WORLD WAR TWO** THAT IT ALL BEGAN. MY RESEARCH TEAM WAS CAPTURED BY NAZI TROOPS DURING A SURPRISE ATTACK!"

"THEY NEEDED SCIENTISTS TO WORK ON A PROJECT TO CHANGE THE DENSITY OF MATTER FOR THE CREATION OF GHOST SOLDIERS OR **WEAPONS** THAT COULD SLIP IN AND OUT OF THE BATTLEFIELD WITHOUT BEING NOTICED...THEY USED **TORTURE** ON US! I...I COULD NOT BEAR IT AND SO, I COMPLIED!"

"THE FIRST TEST WAS ON A **U-BOAT.** BUT THE DEVICE WORKED **TOO** WELL, AND THE VESSEL VANISHED TOTALLY FROM OUR WORLD!"

"BEFORE THE EXPERIMENT COULD BE REPEATED, THE BASE WAS ATTACKED ...I WAS THE **ONLY** SURVIVOR. I STOLE AWAY IN THE NIGHT TO COVER MY TRACKS, AND MY **SHAME!**"

SINCE THEN, I'VE DEVOTED MY LIFE TO ATONING FOR THE **CRIMES** I'VE COMMITTED! I WOULD DO ANYTHING TO REDEEM MYSELF IN THE EYES OF THE STATE!

REDEEM YOURSELF, AFTER WHAT YOU'VE **DONE**?!!

SPINELESS TRAITOR! GIVING IN UNDER A **LITTLE** TORTURE. WHY I'D LIKE A FEW MINUTES WITH YOU **MYSELF**...

AT EASE COMRADE, PHYSICAL INTIMIDATION IS **NEVER** THE ANSWER, EXCEPT UNDER **CERTAIN** CIRCUMSTANCES. HOWEVER, THIS IS NOT ONE OF THEM!

WHATEVER YOUR CRIMES, THE STATE IS ALWAYS READY TO FORGIVE. SO LONG AS YOU COMPLY. NOW TELL ME **WHY** IS THE SUBMARINE ATTACKING OUR STATIONS?

IT MUST BE THE RADIATION... IT'S THE **ONLY** ANSWER!

"THE U-BOAT HAS SAILED THRU THE NETHER WORLDS FOR DECADES! LOST UNTIL NOW..."

"ATOMIC ENERGY FROM OUR PLANTS MUST HAVE PERMEATED THOSE DARK DIMENSIONS AND LED THEM **BACK** TO US!"

UNSEEN BY ALL, THE MARINE MARAUDER **RISES** STEALTHILY INTO THE OFFICE, WITH NO SOUND TO MARK IT'S PASSAGE!

THEY MUST NEED THE POWER TO SOLIDIFY, ALBEIT **BRIEFLY**!

IT MAKES SENSE. OUR STATIONS ARE THE MOST **ADVANCED** ON THE PLANET!

ACH! SO YOU HAFF DISCOVERED OUR **ZECRET** EH? A PITY IT VILL DO YOU NO **GOOT**... **DESTROY ZEM**!!

NAZIS! HERE?!!

5

LOOK! DER KAPTAIN VOS **RIGHT**, ISS HIM! DER ACCURSED **KARNAGE**, VAR HERO OF DER SOVIETS!

LOOKS LIKE YOU'RE **RECOGNISED**, EVEN IN THE SPIRIT WORLD, COMRADE!

JUST WHAT I NEED - A **FAN CLUB**!

SURELY YOU ARE NO **STRANGER** TO RECOGNITION HERR KARNAGE, PARTICULARLY VITH ZOSE WHOM YOU HAFF CROSSED SABRES MIT SO **OFTEN** IN PAST?

YOU!!

KLAUS VON WOLF! THE SCOURGE OF THE SEAWAYS...I MIGHT HAVE KNOWN YOU WERE BEHIND THIS!

YOU TOOK MEIN HAND SHWEIN, BUT MY MASTERS GAVE ME ZIS **CLAW** ZAT I MAY CRUSH YOU VIS IT, UND NOW I **SHALL**!

THE MADMAN'S BOAST SEEMS TO RING TRUE, FOR DESPITE THEIR VALIANT STRUGGLES NEITHER MAN SEEMS ABLE TO MAKE **CONTACT** WITH THEIR SPECTRAL OPPONENTS.

FOOL! YOU CANNOT FIGHT VOT YOU CANNOT **TOUCH**!

OUR HANDS - PASSING **THROUGH** THEM!

VOT A PITY! HOWEFFER IT SEEMS THAT VE, ON THE OZZER HAND, **CAN** TOUCH YOU!!

KARNAGE, THAT'S IT! THEIR **FISTS** ARE SOLID!

OOOOFF!!

COMMUNIST DOG! I VILL - UUUNNNFFF!!

THUNK!

I FOLLOW YOU KOMMISSAR! AND IF WE WORK **TOGETHER**..

6

AND SO THE TIDE OF THE BATTLE **TURNS**, AS SPECTRAL TRICKERY PROVES NO MATCH FOR STATE-HONED REFLEXES AND BLISTERING, BLAZING **LOYALTY**!

KAMERAD! KAMERAD!

SAME OLD NAZI TUNE WHEN THEY REALISE THEY'RE NOT FACING **DEFENCELESS** PEASANTS NOW!

FOOLS! IMBECILES! CAN I TRUST **NO VUN** TO CARRY OUT MEIN ORDERS?! I VILL NOT BE SHTOPPED! NOT BY MERE **COMMUNISTS**!!

WHY CHANGE THE HABITS OF A **LIFETIME** KAPTAIN? THIS IS ONE "MERE COMMUNIST" WHO'S MORE THAN HAPPY TO REMIND YOU OF SOME **OLD TIMES**!

VOT! YOU **DARE**?!!

SURE I DO COMRADE...

BECAUSE **UNLIKE** YOU FASCISTS, WHO OPPRESS THE HUMAN SPIRIT THRU **TYRANNY**, WE COMMUNISTS ALLOW MEN THE FREEDOM TO DARE...AND TO EMBRACE THAT FREEDOM THRU LOYALTY TO THE **STATE**!

OOOFFFFF!!

KLUNK!

I COULDN'T HAVE PUT IT **BETTER** MYSELF COMRADE! NOW LET'S MOP UP THE REST OF THIS GHOSTLY RABBLE!

HISTORY REPEATS ITSELF AS THE **UNSTOPPABLE** FORCES OF THE REICH ARE ONCE MORE DRIVEN INTO CRAVEN FLIGHT...

TEUFEL! VE CANNOT FIGHT THEIR VERDAMMT **UNITY**! FLEE!

NEIN! NOT **AGAIN**! VE CANNOT BE THWARTED AGAIN BY YOU COMMUNISTS. I VILL SINK YOUR **ENTIRE** COUNTRY FOR ZIS!

THE SNARLING THREAT REACHES KEREZOVA, WHO STANDS, **FROZEN** BY WELL DESERVED GUILT!

THEY'RE GOING TO ESCAPE... TO SPREAD MORE TERROR! AND IT'S ALL MY FAULT!

7

IN AN INSTANT KEREZOVA MAKES A **FATEFUL** DECISION AND, WITH GRIM PURPOSE, LEAPS ONBOARD THE SUBMERGING U-BOAT!

WAIT! TAKE ME WITH YOU! TAKE ME WITH YOU!

KEREZOVA! WHAT ARE YOU **DOING**?

KEREZOVA?!! HIMMEL ISS HIM! THE VUN WHO MADE USS LIKE ZIS, **SEIZE** HIM, MACH SCHNELL!!

TOO LATE! THEY'VE GOT HIM, AND NOW HE'S **FADING** OUT LIKE THEM!

ALL HATCHES CLOSE ON THE MARINE MARAUDER AS IT SINKS **DOWN** OUT OF VIEW!

HE'S GONE! BY THUNDER THAT LOUSY TRAITOR, BETRAYING US AGAIN!!

PERHAPS... PERHAPS NOT COMRADE!

AT THAT VERY MOMENT WITHIN THE SINISTER SUBMERSIBLE...

ZO VE MEET **AGAIN** AFFTER ALL ZESE YEARS, VELL NOW YOU CAN FINISH VOT YOU STARTED TRAITOR! TAKE HIM TO ZE GENERATOR!

VIS YOUR **KNOWLEDGE** VE CAN CONTROL OUR DENSITY **VIZZOUT** ZE NEED FOR RADIATION, UND DESTROY WHO VE **CHOOSE**...HAW! HAW!

WHOLE CITIES VILL **BURN** FOR ZE GLORY OF MY **NEW** REICH... UND **EFFEN** ZE AMERICANS VILL HAFF TO ACKNOWLEDGE ME AS A **TRUE** MASTER OF EVIL, OR I VILL **SMASH** ZEIR VERY FOUNDATIONS!!

8

UND YOU VILL **BETRAY** YOUR COUNTRY FOR ME VUNCE **MORE**! OR VILL I HAFF TO...PERSUADE YOU AGAIN?

NO KAPTAIN! I **KNOW** WHAT I MUST DO NOW... WHAT I SHOULD **ALWAYS** HAVE DONE!

AT THE TOUCH OF A SWITCH AN INCREDIBLE TRANSFORMATION BEGINS...

GOTT IN HIMMEL!! VE ARE SOLIDIFYING BEFORE VE CAN **SURFACE**. VE VILL ALL BE DESTROYED... YOU MUST BE **MAD**!!

NOT MAD, JUST A MAN WHO KNOWS HE'S BEEN GIVEN A **SECOND** CHANCE...TO PROVE HIS LOYALTY TO THE STATE!

AND SO MERE SECONDS LATER IN KARNAGE'S OFFICE...

LOOK KOMMISSAR! IT'S **SOLID** NOW. WHAT DOES IT MEAN?

I THINK COMRADE KEREZOVA HAS JUST PAID HIS DEBT IN THE **ONLY** WAY HE COULD!

HMMMP! WELL IF YOU ASK ME THIS WOULD **NEVER** HAVE HAPPENED IN THE FIRST PLACE IF HE HADN'T BEEN SO BLASTED **WEAK**...STILL HE DID THE RIGHT THING IN THE END!

NOW I CAN ONLY SIT BACK AND WAIT FOR THE **NEXT** TRAITOR TO BETRAY THE PEOPLE. THE FIGHT AGAINST SUBVERSION WITHIN OUR **OWN** RANKS GOES ON AS ALWAYS!

NO TRUER WORDS HAVE BEEN SPOKEN LOYAL READERS FOR NEXT ISSUE OUR HERO FINDS HIMSELF FACING THE **INSIDIOUS** POWER OF ORGANISED SUPERSTITION IN **SISTER SINISTER** AND THE ORDER OF THE ROBE! BUY IT ...YOU HAVE **NO** CHOICE!!

9

THE END.

MOSCOW...! CENTRE OF THE FREE WORLD. IT IS HERE THAT MEN CAN WALK IN THE SECURITY THAT ONLY A COMMUNIST REGIME CAN BESTOW!

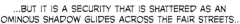

...BUT IT IS A SECURITY THAT IS SHATTERED AS AN OMINOUS SHADOW GLIDES ACROSS THE FAIR STREETS...

THE SOURCE OF THE SHADOW IS A MASSIVE SKY VESSEL OF A DESIGN UNKNOWN TO MAN!

THE AWESOME SHIP LANDS...

IT...IT'S SOME KIND OF **SPACE** SHIP!

BUT **WHERE** DOES IT COME FROM?!!

LOOK! IT'S OPENING UP!

KNEEL, MORTALS...

...KNEEL BEFORE YOUR MASTERS...

...GOG AND MAGOG!!!

THEY'RE **GIANTS!**

1

FROM OUR WORLD OF CENTAURUS 7 WE HAVE COME TO USE THIS PUNY PLANET AS OUR *ARENA!*

IT IS HERE THAT WE SHALL FIGHT TO DETERMINE WHICH OF US SHALL RULE OUR STAR SPANNING *EMPIRE!*

BY ROYAL *DECREE,* YOU WILL ALL VIEW AND LISTEN TO OUR BATTLE USING YOUR PRIMITIVE RADIO AND TELE-VISUAL SYSTEMS!

SAVE YOUR COMMANDS! ONLY THE *STATE* GIVES ORDERS HERE!

THE BEWILDERED BEHEMOTHS TURN TO FIND THEMSELVES FACING THE ASSEMBLED GUARDIANS OF COMMUNISM, THE AWESOME FREEDOM COLLECTIVE AND THEIR SPOKESMAN, THE *KRIMSON KOMMISSAR!*

EH? *WHO* DARES?!!

THIS IS A *COMMUNIST* NATION!

WE DON'T BOW TO OUTDATED IMPERIALIST OPPRESSION COMRADE!

OUTDATED?!! ... YOU *MOCK* OUR EMPIRE?!!

SERVITUDE TO BRUTE FORCE HAS HAD ITS DAY!

ONLY THROUGH UNWAVERING OBEDIENCE TO THE STATE CAN A PEOPLE TRULY ADVANCE!

ER...AH... BAH! YOUR PUNY LOGIC BORES ME! I SHALL SILENCE YOU WITH MY *MIND CONTROL* RAYS!

THAT POWER! KOMMISSAR, I, I CAN'T MOVE!

HERE YOU SHALL REMAIN UNTIL OUR BATTLE IS DONE! THEN *ALL* SHALL SERVE US! *HA HA!*

2

...THE COLLECTIVE!!!

WE GOT HERE JUST IN TIME IT SEEMS!

BUT HOW?!

WHO CARES HOW?! CRUSH them, crush them all for the EMPIRE!

AND SO THE TRUE BATTLE BEGINS! ONE THAT WILL REVERBERATE THROUGH THE VERY HALLS OF ETERNITY!

THE AMAZING MIG-4 IS THE FIRST TO ENTER THE FRAY! ENGAGING HIS OLD FOE THE USURPER!

SURRENDER! YOU CAN'T ESCAPE ME THIS TIME! *

*SEE "WHERE TREASON DWELLS # 9, SMILING SLOANO!

NOT SO FAST MY STEEL STRIPLING! HAVE YOU SO SOON FORGOTTEN MY HYPNO-GOGGLES?!

MASTODON ENNIT? 'EARD YER A BIT OF A TOUGH NUT.

WELL, IN BULLDOG YOU'VE MET YER MATCH! MARQUIS OF QUEENSBURY RULES ...PUT 'EM UP!

HURRR?! ...PUT ..UP?!

HAR! BEST THING ABAT RULES IS 'OW YER BREAK 'EM!

OOOOOFFF!

THOOBM!

5

MEANWHILE *HOMELAND*, SPIRIT OF THE SOIL FACES THE MONSTROUS *LORD HYDE!*

STALACTITE SIMPLETON, YOU THINK A FEW MEASLY BOULDERS CAN STOP *ME?*

BY IMPROVING UPON MY GRANDFATHERS FORMULA, I CAN CHANGE INTO ANY *EVIL* FORM I SO CHOOSE! ...FOR EXAMPLE BY MIXING THESE *TWO* POTIONS...

IN AN INSTANT, THE MASTER OF *HEINOUS TRANSFORMATION* IS GONE, TO BE REPLACED BY...

HA HA! HA! HA! WHAT SAY YOU NOW, MY RECALCITRANT ROCK?!!

C-CRUNCH!

AH! MY DEAR *KOMMISSAR*, I'VE SO WANTED TO SHOW YOU MY AWESOME FIGHTING SKILLS, *GATHERED* FROM EVERY CORNER OF THE EMPIRE!

UNNFF! *STOLEN* YOU MEAN, AND BROADCAST TO YOUR ARMOR BY *ELECTRONIC AUGMENTATION!*

THWOK!

WHAT DOES IT MATTER *HOW* POWER IS GAINED? ONLY HOW IT IS USED... TO *CRUSH* ONE'S LESSERS!

COMMUNISTS ARE NO MAN'S LESSERS! WE WILL *NEVER* SERVE YOU, OR YOUR MISTRESS!

BRITANNIA? HA!.. I'VE ALREADY PLOTTED HER DOWNFALL! ONCE THIS IS ALL OVER *SHE* WILL SERVE *ME!*

AT THAT VERY MOMENT, IN THE HANGMAN'S LAIR, THE SINISTER *TOWER OF LONDON*...

FASTER YOU FOOLS! SEND THE MASTER *MORE* SKILLS!

I... I CAN'T KEEP UP! THE KOMMISSAR IS *TOO* WELL TRAINED!

STOLEN SKILLS CAN NEVER MATCH THOSE *HONESTLY* EARNED! LET'S SEE HOW BRAVE YOU ARE *WITHOUT* YOUR RECEIVER TO PICK UP YOUR "ABILITIES"!

CRUNCH

NOO! PLEASE DON'T HIT ME! I *BEG* OF YOU, I CAN'T STAND PAIN!!

HMMM, IT SEEMS YOUR "COURAGE" WAS BROADCAST *ALONGSIDE* YOUR SKILLS, COMRADE!

MEANWHILE...

AIRBORNE OAF! IT'S USELESS TO RESIST! I CONTROL *ALL* YOU SEE!

BUT I DON'T *NEED* TO SEE COMRADE.

UNNGH!

WHUMP!

NOT WHEN I HAVE *RADAR* TO TELL ME WHAT'S IN *FRONT* OF ME...

BAH! I KNEW THOSE *WEAKLINGS* WOULD FAIL! NO MATTER, I SHALL CRUSH BOTH YOU *AND* YOUR COMRADES BY DUPLICATING YOUR OWN *ROCKY* FORM!

AND THAT... SHALL... BE... YOUR *UNDOING!*

FOR.. I COMMAND.. *ALL* ROCKS.. INCLUDING YOUR.. FISTS.. NOW!

MY *PHIALS!!*

CRASH!

INSTANTLY THE MASTER OF HEINOUS TRANSFORMATION IS POSSESSED BY A MULTITUDE OF GROTESQUE FORMS! EACH MORE BIZARRE THAN THE LAST!

NO! NO! GUUUUUHHH!!

ELSEWHERE, MASTODON DEALS WITH HIS OPPONENT IN A MORE DIRECT FASHION.

HRRRGGGHH!! MASTODON NOT *KNOW* RULES, STUPID ROCK DOG! MASTODON JUST *STRONGEST* ONE THERE IS!!

KA-THOOM!

AS MORTALS BATTLE, SO DO IMMORTALS! *BRITANNIA* MEETS MORE THAN HER MATCH IN THE AWESOME ICE GODDESS *AJYS!*

WHY DO YOU SERVE WITH THESE LOWLY *SLUGS* WHEN THEY SHOULD GROVEL AT YOUR *FEET!*

THE TIME FOR WORSHIP HAS *GONE!*

MORTALS ARE OUR *EQUALS* NOW. NAY, THROUGH *COMMUNISM,* OUR *BETTERS!*

YOUR DAY ALSO HAS PASSED *BRITANNIA!*

IT IS TIME FOR YOU TO JOIN THE *OLD* GODS IN THE HALLS OF DARKNESS NOW!

IN THE NAME OF *THE PEOPLE AND THE STATE,* I BID YOU BEGONE!

NOOOO!

FINALLY...

THAT'S THE LAST OF THEM, AND THEIR PLAN!

INDEED YOUNG ONE! A PLAN THAT *ALMOST* SUCCEEDED!

WHAT *NOW* KOMMISSAR?

SENDING THEM BACK TO THE MERCY OF THEIR LONDON MASTERS SHOULD BE *PUNISHMENT* ENOUGH, COMRADE!

BUT OUR PLOT WAS *PERFECT.* HOW DID YOU UNCOVER IT?!

8

HOW TO DRAW COMICS THE KREMLIN WAY

CHAPTER SEVENTY-THREE: STATE APPROVED PENCIL LAYOUTS

AS EVERY ASPIRING STATE ARTIST KNOWS, WE HERE AT KREMLIN PRIDE OURSELVES ON OUR DYNAMIC, YET ACCURATE LAYOUTS. HERE IS JUST ONE EXAMPLE OF OUR STRINGENT STANDARDS IN OPERATION.
IF YOU LOYAL FANS TAKE A LOOK AT HIS DEFTLY YET INACCURATELY RENDERED PANEL HERE, YOU WILL DOUBTLESS NOTICE A FEW GRIEVOUS ERRORS.

WITHIN MERE MINUTES, THE FEARLESS *FREEDOM COLLECTIVE* SECURE THE *ENTIRE* BUILDING...

A *YANKEE* ASSASSIN!

IT WAS *FORTUNATE* THAT YOU WERE ABLE TO *STOP* HIM IN TIME KOMMISSAR!

I WAS ONLY DOING MY *DUTY* FOR THE PEOPLE, COMRADES!

YOU'VE GUESSED IT TRUE FOLLOWERS: THE OTHER TWO FIGURES IN THE PANEL ARE NOT THERE. IN FACT THEY WERE **NEVER** THERE... UNDERSTAND?

NOW THAT THE WRITER, PENCILLER, INKER AND LETTERER HAVE ALL BEEN SENT TO OUR SIBERIAN STUDIOS FOR SOME MUCH NEEDED RE-TRAINING, A NEW TEAM TACKLES THE PROBLEM WITH SOME POLITBURO WHITE AND ALMOST GET IT RIGHT... ALMOST! CAN THE MOST TRUSTWORTHY AMONGST YOU SPOT **THEIR** MISTAKE?

THAT'S RIGHT! THE POSITION OF OUR GREAT LEADER IN THE PREVIOUS PANEL WAS NOT APPROPRIATE FOR A MAN OF HIS STATURE. THIS NEW PANEL BELOW IS NOW FINISHED BY YET ANOTHER TEAM, WHILE THOSE INCOMPETENT BUNGLERS HAVE BEEN SENT TO JOIN THEIR PREDECESSORS.

WELL THAT'S ANOTHER LESSON FOR OUR LOYAL YOUNG READERS TO REMEMBER. AT KREMLIN IT PAYS TO GET YOUR CRAFT RIGHT, A TRUTH MANY OF OUR EX-EMPLOYEES CAN ATTEST TO. NOW TURN THE PAGE FOR THE NEXT CHAPTER ON HOW TO SPOT SUBVERSIVE INKING.

**BE PART OF THE
ROUGH CUT COMICS
COMMUNITY**

FOLLOW US ON FACEBOOK:
www.facebook.com/roughcutcomicsuk

ON TWITTER
twitter.com/roughcutcomics

ON PINTEREST
pinterest.com/roughcutcomics/

THE ROUGH CUT COMICS BLOG
http://roughcutcomics.blogspot.co.uk/

OUR WEBSITE:
www.roughcut-comics.com

A People's Champion who gave his all for the State named the Krimson Kommissar; the Siberian ice goddess Ajys; the daredevil Soviet pilot who transformed into the man, half jet-plane MIG-4; the mighty spirit of the Russian soil named Homeland; and the monstrous Mastadon. Separately, they are extraordinary individuals. But together, they are the Freedom Collective – Communism's Mightiest Super-Heroes. This is the first volume of their original adventures from the milestone Soviet publishing house Kremlin Comics ... reprinted here in the west by Rough Cut Comics, Bah!

ISBN 978-0-9546726-

ISBN: 0-9546726-

9 780954 672652